D.A.M.

DIET ATTITUDE
MEDITATION

D.A.M.

DIET ATTITUDE MEDITATION

By

Gayle Schilz and Edgar Cayce

DIET— A STATE OF MIND

ATTITUDE — CHANGING THE NEGATIVE INTO POSITIVE

MEDITATION — AS THE RIVER THAT NEVER STOPS FLOWING YOUR ENERGY WILL FLOW LIKE WATER

EDGAR CAYCE IS A BIG PART IN MY LIFE AS HE CAME TO ME IN A DREAM

ACKNOWLEDGEMENTS

It did not take long to write the book after my husband died, but I got so busy volunteering keeping active in the community. Then I thought this world is only a material world not spiritual world.

I thought people could change their diet, attitude and meditate and it became D.A.M. Changing the negative into positive. So I contemplated on it and put it into action, knowing that they are angels thoughts flowing from God to man, so act on them.

I want to thank my mom for her efforts and I am grateful for a friend who put me on the path to EDGAR CAYCE.

I want those to know I am grateful for sharing their thoughts with me.

On 10 - 31-94 Edgar Cayce came to me in a dream.

Again I could not have done it without the help from God. It was his intelligence that came through me.

"WAKE UP"

THIS WORLD IS ONLY AN ILLUSION

I bet you thought Dam this is going to be a great book.

Well, it is. Turning the negative into positive.

Diet

Attitude

Meditation

This book can be a stepping stone toward a more positive life and attitude.

If you think your life is great and happy now it is only a sample of what your life can really be.

Some people search for Self through drugs. Famous writers on self-discovery are psychologically confused, don't be fooled. What ever you are aiming for, read books on spiritual and personal growth and yoga, read books that are written and practiced by what they preach.

You have the power to change your environment; anything around you presents suggestions to your imagination. You affect your environment.

"No matter what we do or become, we are still the self."

The universe is waiting to give you everything you need!

Be aware of your self.

Forward

People have been searching all their life for something, now is the time to turn within.

When you relax, your body you will unfold like a flower opening up to the sun, taking in all the beauty and love that it gives.

Over twenty five years ago, when I was working, I stopped myself and said there has to be more to life then just getting up in the morning, going to work, having dinner parties, going out.

Strutting with peacocks at night and walking with the turkeys in the morning. That is when I started to do yoga and meditate.

I just want to share with you the knowledge and universal insights and wisdom I have experienced in the past and now. I know you can experience the same.

What was hid shall be revealed. There are no secrets in life. Knowledge should be for free. Everything comes from within and from God.

I think of this world as a beautiful garden and everyone in it is a beautiful flower.

I asked God, who is this great being who is going to walk this earth plane when the new kingdom of Brotherhood comes. He answered me.

I saw him coming I saw him in a dream, he is beautiful Jesus Christ.

There is a purpose why we are here and only God has the answer. We are all in our right place and this moment contains our life.

We are a reflection of this world and what you see in others is a reflection of the self.

Have a more understanding of the self and your true identity don't ever lose it.

You picked birth and you have to live it out, so why not do it with grace and love.

In God's kingdom everything is perfect and so are you. Become one with God and the universe.

Time goes by so fast it will never return, so forget the past it is dead, now is the time for you to go on your journey and illumine the world.

Let truth, light and love pour out from your heart. Let forgiveness be in every soul. Let this world be restored to sanity. Let this be the beginning of peace and Brotherhood. So be it.

We need a great change to find our way back to God and the force that brought us here. The truth makes all things possible.

We can change this world from a material world to a spiritual world.

If you want to change your life, the time is Now! Turning your negative thoughts into positive ones.

Be liberated. Search for the experience of God. Only good will come from it. God will change your life and make it what he chooses to overcome all obstacles with unshakable resolve.

'Just think how a few words can change your life'

Through this book and through a good teacher, you too can gain great powers. As long as it is spiritual, natural, nature.

Many powers develop through yoga, through specific techniques. These powers must be accepted as part of our omnipresent and omnipotent nature. Do not play games with the phenomena.

There was a yogi who attained great powers through disciplined practices. This pseudo-yogi sensed power and became arrogant and dominating. A little bird disturbed his meditation. He looked at the bird with malice in his eyes the bird fell to the ground dead. On his wanderings, he came to this house and shouted and demanded hospitality (it is practice in India to treat yogis with hospitality). There was no reply. He shouted louder. Awhile later, a woman came to the door, the yogi glared at her, but nothing happened. She spoke calm and serene saying, "See I am not like that little bird who shrivelled up when you looked at him." "How do you know, this was many miles away"; the yoga was disillusioned. She replied "I too, have many powers I achieved them through the practices that you follow. I have the powers because I have faithfully, concentratedly and selflessly served my husband who has been ill and incapacitated for many years." The yogi learned a great lesson.

The real power is spiritual power

ON 10-31-94 Edgar Cayce came to me in a dream and he said real loud bless this county and were you live, I opened my eyes and I felt his presents leaving the room right next to my bed, I looked at the clock it was 6:30 a.m. this day the people around the world pray for peace. I wrote the A.R.E. clinic to let them know and they were happy to here this and they were going to share it with others.

The reason Edgar Cayce said it so loud is because I tell God please make things loud and clear for me.

Diet

Character is molded by the type of food we take and how we eat it. Some people live to eat than eat to live.

This brings civilized man's greatest sins-the temperature of food and drink.

A tired body has a tired stomach. Food gives strength and food will serve to strength our anger.

When you are born, you are born with a certain amount of nourishment to last to the end of your days. If you consume this food too quickly, we die earlier, the less you eat the longer you live.

Food only has the power that you give it.

Diet and exercise. Take the time to listen to your body. It is talking to you.

Some people get indigestion before they eat.

It isn't what you eat, it's what you eat mentally.

It isn't what goes into the mouth, it's what comes out of the mouth.

Food is only ordinary matter but it carries the feelings of the person who made it.

Food reflects our attitude toward life. When we change our food habits our life changes also. When you want more food fill your belly with love.

As the sun melts the snow away, you can melt the fat away with your thoughts.

Before you eat bless your food and offer it to God. Eat in silence or if you talk, talk about good things nothing to upset you. You want your food to be relaxed. Put your fork down until your next bite, or use your fingers, it shows character. Chew your food ten times on each side of your mouth.

When you eat don't swallow your food in chunks, it can make you heavier.

You lose a lot of energy from eating and talking.

The desires for food. Think of all the money spent on food in the world and it is only matter.

Remember the Garden of Eden. Live in paradise and not eat the fruit of the tree of knowledge of good and evil.

Man is the connecting link between spirt and matter.

Hunger is natural. Appetite is unnatural. It's just a wish to overstimulate the palate, we overburden our organs and make the body sick. Civilized man becomes accustomed to this unnatural way of eating and drinking that is why there is so much unhappiness and disease in the world.

Think of the reports of over 78,000,00 people overweight. The billions of dollar industry to fight fat. The millions in exercise equipment the money in legal diet pills millions in diet food. The millions in diet books. The use of powerful drugs may reduce the weight but do damage to your health.

You cannot keep up even health if you remain inactive!

People with a depraved appetite for food, drugs, and tobacco destroy the Minds Mastery. You have to gain divine strength and understanding; there is no enjoyment to fill yourself with all these things and act like a fool.

Suffering inconceivably is terrible to man's self-respect. It is a lack of weakness and no control over the self. It is unnatural and unattractive free yourself of these things don't be a servant. You are master over the senses, know you are complete and satisfied.

Today some blame obesity on psychological or emotional state. It is your problem if you don't handle it, it will handle you.

People use a lot of excuses to over eat, drink instead of facing the problem, and facing their own true self.

Obesity is the greatest danger to your health, food is the substance of physical existence.

Why are people over weight, overeating, under exercising?

You can shed unwanted weight, fattening foods and the compulsion of overeating. Use your self-control tell yourself and see yourself as slim and fit. You will feel great losing excess weight. Feel full and satisfied with smaller portions. Drink more water before eating. Fill your belly with love in between meals. Drink an ounce of grape juice and an ounce of water before each meal and before you go to bed. Drink a cup of joy mentally.

See yourself healthy and your appearance the way you saw yourself before you gained the weight. Stop the junk foods, have self-control and stick to a healthy diet.

Take a picture and put it up so you see it every day. A picture that you were less heavy. Know that this is the way you want to look like now.

Some people eat to satisfy their own greed just enough for survival. They wonder why nature laughs at them.

Our bodies are constructed of the foods we eat. Vegetation captures red light from the sun and stores it. This light is released in the body during the process known as oxidation. Our body is constructed of light and our muscles run off red sunlight.

We take liquids because No-no life can manifest without water. We take gases in through the nose which is used for oxygen. The most important of all is prana (energy) all food is a form of the human body is capable of changing one form of energy into another. For breath is life.

Over eating, you can lose the magnetism from the saints.

Fasting

People fast for a number of reasons. To overcome the craving for food. Fasting is a self-discipline by reducing solid food intake. Fasting breaks down protein in the body cells, Fasting removes toxins from the body, Fasting helps to rid certain diseases or other problems.

Be more concerned what comes out of the mouth than what goes in.

Don't take any poisons like Greed, Anger, and Ignorance of truth, of impermanence, which is the root of the other two. In a fulfilled life anger becomes compassion, and greed becomes wisdom.

Yoga

Grace reveals the secrets of yoga and the mysteries of our own life in this world. Through grace, we experience the divine light and merge into love. Through this experience, we will meet again and again.

Within each human being lies a supreme power called Kundaline (energy). Once awakened, you experience your own divinity and the world around us and our life becomes transformed. Union of oneness with the self, with God.

Miracles happen through yoga. Yoga is the oldest science of man. The word yoga means to bind or yoke; the yoking of all powers of the body, mind and soul to God. Yoga is a disciplined ancient system which teaches men how to know himself. Like any other science, yoga has divided into many specialized areas of practice. The main branches of yoga are known as Hatha Yoga, which is the study of the body. Raja Yoga which is the study of the mind. Karma Yoga, yoga of action, Juana Yoga, the yoga of knowledge, Bhakti Yoga, people with inflated egos. Bhahti yoga is a method of tranacending the ego by devoted services. When you love other people, then you are able to love yourself, then you can truly love God's non-self ego.

There is nothing easier to be than what you are already.

The state of yoga requires no effort to be realised. It requires letting go of all effort to be something other than what you really are. That is the cause of all your problems.

The image a man makes of himself is called the ego.

God said "let us make man in our image." Do you see that image today?

Mantra Yoga, transcending all thoughts and concepts to experience the undefinable, inconceivable, reality-the self by stopping all thinking.

Raja Yoga, is the supreme yogalthe self that I am, that I am. To live in the world of confusion and ignorance and yet be untouched by it, discover the true selves.

Tantra Yoga, a person who lives in awareness of the creative power of the imagination, when it chooses escapism rather than facing up to the world.

The imagination can cure incurable diseases.

Ashtanga Yoga, is a yoga, a way of life. It involves the personality it is the practice of all the branches of yoga at once. Happiness and fulfilment are their reasons for living.

Yogha is from the west. The Indian already obtained highly realistic estimate of the age of the universe. The thing about traditional yoga has been tried and tested over and over for thousands of years. The knowledge has been handed down by the word of mouth.

It is written in Sanskrit. Sanskrit is the language of Yoga. Sanskrit means Mathematically and Scientifically.

Guru (Master)

Get acquainted with your body.

Hatha Yoga is to bring optuem health and well being to each individual. The student is taught to know his body and take care of his physical self by following a daily routine of poses.

Yoga is practised at the highest level.

Yoga is not a religion in itself. It is a way of life, you can attain a deeper fuller understanding of your own religion.

Prevention of disease is possible only if we follow the important yogic rules. Health, proper exercise, proper breathing exercise to absorb more oxygen, proper relaxation of the body and mind, natural wholesome food and proper thinking and concentration of the mind.

Yoga tones the body and gives you more energy, vitality, and an over all improvement in good health and looks. Since Hatha Yoga is the science of understanding the human form, it reaches a much deeper depth of knowing how to preserve the health and youthfulness of one's self.

Through the postures tension will be released along the nerves creating a balance between the left and right sides of the body, this will eliminate undue stress, because it reacenters the body structure.

Pills don't work, yoga does.

It is only through yoga that you will gain the knowledge to create the happy and healthy body and mind.

A yogis life is not measured by his days, but the breaths he takes, slow and deep breathing.

Mind is the master of the senses and the breath is master of the mind.

Prãnãyãma is a science of breath (Drana) (energy) prana the breath of life, the lord of the mind. The hub which the wheel of life revolves. Prãnãyãma is a sanskrit word for breathing. Breath prana is rhythic control of the breath. It brings inner peace and changes the mental outlook on you. It reduces cravings of your senses, like worldly pleasures, smoking, drinking and sexual indulgence.

Kundalina (energy) this energy lies dormant in the lower part of the spine. Once you arouse this energy you experience true bliss.

Pursue yoga to purify your discrimination and hatred will loosen it's hold.

Don't get the false impression that the yogi is a person who is withdrawn from the world. He is a great manifester of life; he is an example how life can be lived to obtain fulfilment and bring happiness to everyone around. If you do yoga, your life will change. People around you will notice.

You have to go to yoga, it will not come to you. You can start yoga at any age any time. You are the creator of your own needs. Ask God to transform you completely.

There are great changes taking place throughout the entire world. Mankind is faced with problems. Things are speeding up. People are hardening themselves; people are more selfish and cut off from others. We need the beginning of a new age of harmony, creativity and happiness.

May the outward and inward man be at one.

Shanti (peace)

A short story

When I was Nine years old, I was roller skating with my Sister and I needed the skate key and she said. "If you want it, chase me." I did, I fell and hit my mouth on the cement curb. My mouth opened up and my teeth were pushed up in my gums, I had passed out. When I came to, I did not even know my own Sister. I ran home and my parents took me to the Dentist.

Three months later I started to get seizures. I had tests taken and I was told I had Epilepsy. For years I was on medication but it did not stop me from doing anything. I was told I would outgrow it by the time I was Eighteen. At Eighteen I stopped the medication and the seizures were not that bad, since I was to outgrow it. My peers use to make fun of me. When I was in my Twenties, I had less and less seizures but I started to black out with no warning, so I went for help at this one hospital noted for Epilepsy. I was told after some tests I was to have brain surgery, but after these three doctors came into the room and talked to me, it was like a Three ring circus.

I left the hospital. A week later I passed out again so I went to this other hospital and this doctor told me we have all new kinds of medication for epilepsy. He gave me seventeen different pills to take and pain pills because I had this bump on my head from when I fell with blacking out.

I went home and took all the pills and that night in bed my heart started to beat so fast I thought I was having a heart attack. I called this doctor and I told him how I felt and he said "you were thinking of me that is why my heart was beating so fast." I went back to see him and he wanted to give me more pills, and he wanted to adopt me.

I passed out again at home and was taken to the hospital. I did not wake up until three days later. My family was told I was never going to come out of it and to get ready to prepare for a funeral.

When I was leaving the hospital, this doctor told me he wanted me to come back for a visit. I went back and while I was sitting in the waiting room I looked at that people sitting there and all I saw was people who looked like zombies. Thinking this man wants to adopt me and he has a wife and a little child. I called my lawyer and told him and I said I was never going back. I turned to God and nature for help and this one clinic that is noted for all great things and natural.

I never took another pill since then when I felt I was going to have a seizure I denied it, I stayed with what this clinic told me, like no extra salt or fruit at night and I kept on with my yoga which I kept feeling stronger. Later on a friend that I met told me I could have used spiritual healing to bring back the energy that I lost. I got a reading for the A. R. E. clinic. Edgar Cayce to rid myself of epilepsy. I had been asking God to dissolve my epilepsy and he heard me. I was doing the cobra in yoga and as I was coming up in the pose I was in, all of a sudden I knew I was free from epilepsy. I called the doctor and I asked him to take all the tests and he did and he called me back and said congratulations you don't have epilepsy. I wanted to say I know, but this doctor knew I stayed on a spiritual path and health is natural.

I thought why not write a book, so I did and I donated that book to the A. R. E. Clinic Edgar Cayce

I was even on T.V. and I still remember this one person from T.V. said to me "are you the people that run around the streets foaming at the mouth?" He just showed his ignorance.

Since then I have learned to deny sickness and disease.

I always felt someone from the spiritual world was with me when I wrote that book

Attitude

Attitude has everything to do with your life and the world around you.

Your thoughts are very powerful so be careful how you use them. Life is a symbol of love. Mind is the source of all movement.

You don't have to change the world change yourself. Start each day with a positive mental attitude. Be filled with strength and courage. Today is a great day to be optimistic and filled with enthusiasm. Every day of your life will bring new opportunities. Divine love will meet all your human needs and supply will be abundant and your work belongs to you and no one else can do it. Don't let any negative thought stay with you for even a moment. It will bring all kinds of disease and difficulty.

You are a great being and nothing evil can enter your day unless you give it the power to hurt you. Evil thoughts reach no farther or can do no harm than one's belief permit them to.

You are the master over your sense. You have divine mind and divine power to do anything.

Have you kept the faith today?

At the end of the day, you feel like you are losing it, STOP. Call on God to send you an angel. Use your subconscious mind that natural energy will rise from the surface. Supercharge yourself, feeling energized and refreshed. Don't let your senses lose sight. Don't panic. God is working wonders for you. Everything is perfect and harmonious right now.

Let no one tempt, harm, or control you. You are master of the occasion. You are not weak or lacking confidence.

Be honest and truthful. Honesty is divine power. Stand your ground with truth and love and you will win.

Love your enemies and God will surely come looking for you.

Don't doubt yourself or feed your fears. Attitude is a state of mind. Your attitude is not your true being. There is only good in the self no matter what anyone ever did. There is good in everyone. Just know it is not their true being.

People have fears and when you feed those fears, they get bigger and bigger. You hear so much on the news today, how buildings are being blown up with people inside, or those who are being killed, etc. It is only matter and they are already home with God.

'We can't be destroyed.' Jesus Christ proved it to us. That the body is only matter.

No matter what goes on in this world, it is not our concern. Just take charge of your own life and keep your own slate clean. God is an operation. They are God's laws, not ours.

All that we are is the result of what we have thought. Nothing shows a man's character more than what he laughts at.

Some people don't take the time for God but have time for everything else. They turn to God at the last moment. If they would have turned to God before, they could have avoided a lot of pain discomfort.

Some people have a bad disposition and have a lot of anger they won't let go of. If you hurt others or curse people out it will cause you to have all kinds of illnesses and diseases. It will show on your body. Next time you see someone with a cold or illness, you might think to yourself what were his or her thoughts. This may want you to think of watching your thoughts more.

You block the flow of circulation to eliminating channels. Think of your channels being filled with truth and love.

Heart attacks are blockages that you have been hanging onto from a past life. The blockages you have, are from not letting go.

I used to kid my husband and tell him all the time, "what did you do in your past life", because it is catching up with you in this life time.

We are all individuals. We all have our own thoughts. Anger can destroy you. Hate blinds the eyes. Don't burn your mind in jealousy. Never show anger or hate to anyone or it will come back to you. Don't let anger upset you. There is more power in tenderness than anger. Work on forgiveness and love not anger. Don't worry about others' health problems or loved ones. Why worry. When you pray, know the power from the creative force. Have faith in God and yourself that all will go well. What ever you do, do it without harm to your self.

You have that divine power within you to be spiritually minded and mentally heal them and yourself.

Do not give people the power to hurt you. No matter what anyone says about you, as long as you know the truth in your heart. You gain control over the mind.

Don't think "I am" sick. I am going to always be sick" You may have a physical body but you have to have a spiritual mind, divine mind and divine love, to heal you.

We are a reflection of God. All God made was good.

People are sick because they are unhappy or they have a variety of stress, hatred, fear, wrong thinking about illness. Be relaxed and calm and let the healing energy flow through you. Health is natural.

Have faith everything is all right.

This world we live, in is an energy field. We all have an aura around us. So think of God surrounding you with protective forces of love, peace and harmony and that you are protected from all negativity; that this aura repels negativity and peace and love surround you.

All healing comes from God and from within. Change your attitude and let the life force become constructive not destructive. Don't poison the mind. You have the capacity to change the self. The moment you have a negative thought, change it to positive. You have the will to do it. Know that.

Don't be discouraged, have courage within the self. All healing divine love will heal situations that seem impossible.

Being something other than what we really are, is the cause of all our problems.

There is a cure for everyone. Our imagination can cure incurable diseases.

If you want something in life and you cannot have it, think about a few minutes and then forget about.

What ever you do in life, don't wait for praise. Thank yourself.

Just as a person has a business, etc. It may be always wants more. The more you have, the more you have to lose.

Don't criticize others or yourself. Just see beauty, order, peace and honesty.

When you work, think of work as worship. When you are with your co-workers and have odds with them or a family member, inhale your love to them and exhale your love to them. It may kill you to do it, but you will feel better and they will come to you.

If you are not happy with your work then do something else. It isn't what you do as long as you are happy doing it.

Some people set their affections on material things and love the material and trust in it, than the spiritual. This is a material world not spiritual.

Get rid of material things and keep only what you need. We are only here for a short time then you won't have to worry about losing anything. Your treasures are in heaven. Live on what is allotted to you.

We all have duties to fulfill in this life. We are only residents and when we die we won't be anything what we thought we were, while we were here. This is God's world. Don't be attached to it or this body or this earth plane. Just perform your duties without being identified with them. Know that you are free.

What you focus on, you create and the company you keep creates your destiny. When you think from the smallest to the biggest wrong thoughts of others and you know it is wrong and they are hurting you, they are only hurting themselves. But they will suffer in health unless they change their thoughts.

Don't be your own enemy. It will, it will, bring torture. Don't use God as an excuse for your own mistakes.

Some people are so in love with their thoughts that no one else counts.

People say why me? Why do I have all these problems. Take a good look at yourself and your life. Just the smallest thing may affect you and your life.

It could cause some kind of illness or disease. Yes, it is true, it takes a lot of self control and discipline every moment every day. At the end of the day take inventory, what you did, how much good, how much you disliked of yourself and your attitude.

Were you happy what you did or not?

Burn the records of the day and start fresh and new. Start fresh and new always with a new moon.

Make a circle like a pie, and put it into sections. See how much time throughout the day, you spent, on family, work, fun, rest exercises and spiritual. "Work on it."

Turn your past and future over to God,

Everything in the past died yesterday. Everything in the future was born today.

Take one minute of every hour to repeat God's name. It will put you on a higher spiritual plane.

Breathe in truth and breathe out love.

Love inspires and illuminates our way. Go within and become one with God.

Just as past failures repeat themselves, you will be a better person from it; from the mistakes you make.

Failure is a stepping stone toward future success.

Don't judge others. Judge yourself.

Mistakes are blessings and we can learn from them. They will never happen again. We just have to listen and move ahead.

If anything goes wrong, don't waste time or energy on it. Don't be concerned. You are not accountable for others mistakes. The battle is not yours but God's. Just keep your own slate clean.

Free yourself from any guilt you are hanging onto; don't blame others or yourself.

Start new right now, with love and peace and tranquility. Keep positive thoughts that it is all dissolved.

What ever you do, do it for yourself. Free yourself from stress. Tell yourself you are relaxed and free; that your senses remain clear and alert what ever you do. Let anxiety and stress roll off like the beads on the back of a duck.

Bring more laughter into your life, keep a good sense of humor. Laughing is fun and therapeutic, see the humor in life. Share your laughter. Smile and laugh more often.

Get rid of inverted thoughts, keep positive ones. Have the power to program your life to make it happy and successful. Thinking positive beliefs and attitudes. Accept everything as is. Fill your life with positive experiences.

Control your time so it does not control you. Organize your time to create extra hours in the day. Become more efficient and organized. Tell yourself you are highly organized and you can complete tasks more quickly.

Today people and children want to win. Winning is a state of mind. You can use the power of your subconscious mind to increase your endurance and strength and your coordination. Fill yourself with positive feelings of confidence. You can win.

If you try too hard it is beyond reach.

No matter what your circumstances are, maintain a calm tolerance. Have patience understanding and everyone around you will be calm too.

Admit your fears. It's a weakness, recognize it as such. Be free of fear and worry. Place your negative thoughts with positive ones; be calm and confident. God plans our life. When you let go, it all works out for the best.

It is just a dream and someday you will awake from it.

If everyone thought blue skies and sunshine, we would have it all the time.

When people go to warmer climates because of their health, they come back with the same illness until next year. They keep that thought all year round. (Good excuse for a vacation every year) It is fear of holding on. It's a blockage. You have to let go and no, it is not your true self.

It isn't the change, it is the thought. People spend a lot of money to feel better but they can be cured right where they are. Every year you hear the same thing, it's flu time or colds. They coincide themselves all year.

Create in yourself a paradise. Be satisfied in thought. Again, change the negative into positive right away so it does not bring you any sort of disease or difficulty. Having divine love will heal.

Each man must discover his own way in life and that way lies in his heart.

Let man dwell into the depths of his being, his true center is not far from him.

34

Let your actions be led by yourself not by events.

He who knows others is wise, but he who knows himself is enlightened.

Karma, Your past and future experiences. You have no karma. You're one with spirit if you realize the truth, even if you think you are a mortal being, but in back of your mind you are God, you are free.

Some people have this big ego trip or are born out of an inferior complex. Don't let the ego get in the way or it will control you. Take charge of your life. Do not lose your true identity.

Think more of God than yourself. Man is wrapped up in material things. He forgot where he came from. This is God's kingdom and he is in control.

When thoughts arise, then do all things arise. When thoughts vanish then do all things vanish.

Nature teachers us to love man.

Progress is only what we can fulfill. Man walks where he looks, where his treasures are there is his heart.

Believe all things are possible. Get rid of the fear or problem you are hanging on to. We have endless opportunities. All we have to do is listen and move ahead.

Selfishness, all pain and suffering are results of want of harmony and the one terrible and only cause of the disturbance of harmony is selfishness, in some form or another.

Control; You think you are in control; you think you have power; your powerless power over nothingness. God is in control and gives us divine power; divine mind, the power to do anything. What ever we do and as long as it is good cause, God only knows good; everything else is evil.

Any thought that you have, God already had that thought.

You are never alone. God is always with you. Don't punish yourself and great things will happen.

We choose to take birth on this earth plane so we have to live it out. This world doesn't have to change, we do. Change yourself now! have freedom not enslavement.

As the soil, however rich it may be, cannot be productive without culture, so the mind without cultivation can never produce good fruit.

Heavy thoughts bring on physical maladies.

When the soul is oppressed so is the body.

When you go to a doctor, he should mentally heal you, so at the first visit you are healed. Sick people sometimes know more than their doctors support their trust.

If you have a problem, what ever it may be, stand your ground with truth and love and you will win.

The only medicine that you need is the mind. Mind is medicine. Know the truth that you can mentally heal yourself. Know the truth about yourself so you can face yourself every day. Focus on the truth and belive it.

Nothing can enter your mind unless you let it or give people the power to hurt you. People who think they have power, are powerless. Reverse your thoughts. God only has good in store for you. Bless others and you will blessed. Think good of yourself and others, as no one is greater than the next.

Human love is doubt and fear, but is God's love who loves man, not man's love.

Don't be conformed to this world, be transformed.

Love will cast out all fear. We will succeed if we believe in what we are doing is right.

Repeat love 100 times a day or say, "Every day in every way, I am getting better and better through the grace of God through a positive mental attitude."

When you stop doubting yourself, you will have everything you need, know you are strong enough, wise enough, loving enough, to never doubt yourself again.

When you remove all your negative thoughts, everything becomes love. We are all God's children; accept everyone as is. God is our Father, Mother, Friend, and Brother. Your wealth he is all.

Start every day to worship God and yourself, as the sun and moon give us a message every day. We came from light.

I saw myself in a dream. I was above this blue water, then I saw myself in light form. I walked away, disapeared, vanished. Then I saw myself in the physical form with this aura around me. When you see these visions and of Jesus Christ and God, know you are one with God and keep them in your heart.

You can heal yourself and others if you are a thousand miles away. Mentally just keep your thoughts on the healing that they are special and perfect light right now.

There are ways of healing and know God fills every space with love. You are his perfect child and God's laws are meant to bring joy to you, not suffering.

God does not hold us accountable for the action of others. Don't worry what goes on in this world; it is God's battle not ours. Everything will come to pass.

If you don't see good in others or yourself, it is an insult to God. Keep your hands busy and your mind on God.

We are all connected in some way. Don't look at faults in others, or judge others. Judge yourself.

Do not see people with the physical eye, see them with your spiritual eye.

The cycle of life and death. A person who knows the self, both life and death, can become enjoyable games. You have to liberate yourself from fear of death. We will leave everything behind and go to God. We shouldn't fear death, but accept it with courage. Death is nothing more than a long sleep.

It is our destiny and we have control over it.

Death can be a bad marriage, divorce, poverty, lies, fear, etc. Age is mortality eternal; age is all there is forever. Age is a slow death. There is no being or end with God.

Once you rid yourself of all fears, you will be healed.

We reap the consequences of our actions.

When we look into a mirror and do not like what we see, that is an insult to God.

Contemplate who am I. You are the self.

Walk by faith not by sight.

Believe, know the truth, all things are possible. All others things will pass away.

Love yourself and be at peace.

Take charge of your life and you and your thoughts will be able to do anything.

Life is without beginning or end. Eternity is forever infinite.

If you cover up your negative thoughts you will not prosper. If you give them to God you will bear fruit.

Just as heaven and hell is a state of mind. If you do good, you will feel good. If you do bad, you will feel bad.

Change your concept of living, and the way you think daily, what ever you do.

Throughout, the day, whereever you go, think good of others and yourself. Keep your mind on only good and on God. Know that when you travel or in a car etc., think thoughts like God is ahead of you, guiding you each step of the way.

When you enter your home or anyone elses, know that this home is filled with perfect love and no evil can enter. Bless this home and everyone in it.

When you enter your home, take your shoes off. This way you leave one world and enter into another.

Hang your problems up when you hang your coat up. Better yet, don't bring your problems home. Give them to God.

You cannot see the beauty outside unless you have beauty on the inside. You cannot understand beauty unless you yourself are beautiful on the inside.

Have faith and confidence in yourself. Be free of fear and worry. Change negative thoughts to positive right away. You can always handle any situation as long as you stay calm and relaxed. Be confident and secure.

People who are not satisfied with their lives, turn to drugs, alcohol or suicide, which is not a way out. As you will not be happy on the next plane, because it will still be in your thoughts, when you really see yourself.

You have to face your own true self now. You have to be loved and nurtured back to health and your true being. Believe in yourself that you are loved and to be loved; other wise you are not loving. You are full of love and

43

acceptance. Except yourself unconditionally. You are lovable.

What ever enslaves man, know the truth and you will be free.

Do not worship your personality. Do not take thought for your life.

What we need is prayer and desire, growth, grace and love. Good deeds, our debt to God and gratitude for all he has done for us.

You have the power within you to change your negative thoughts toward so positive attitude.

Put God first in your life. Center your life around God and everything else will follow.

Know every day we are living in the light of God, surrounded by his love and surrounded by the divine light and it's all healing powers.

'Seeing my loved one as an angel'

Before my husband's life energy ran out, I knew nine months before, that great things would be happening in my life and they are not only for myself but for others.

Everything now is coming from God, is supremely natural.

My husband was twenty years older than me, but our age did not mean anything. I just think of being ageless.

We had been together just about thirty years. He was successful in the restaurant business.

Ten years before he died, he had a lot of health problems. I dream't three nights before he went to the hospital, two nights in a row, that I saw priests and nuns and this room number. I knew if he would be in this wing, he would die.

It was a very hot day in August. We were out for the day and I started to get dinner ready. He was washing up for dinner when all of a sudden he was in a lot of pain. He said it felt like knives were in his back. He went on the bed and he was just thrusting back and forth.

He started to sweat. The water was pouring out of him from the pain. Then he could not breath, so I called for help. When the men came to help him, they said it was a broken back or an aneurysm. I new it was not a broken back, but all I could think of, it has to be an aneurysm and people have less than a minute to live.

They transported him to the hospital and gave him fifteen milligrams of morphine. It took only five minutes to get to the hospital and I was told they thought he would never make it.

At the hospital, all the staff were working on him and one of the doctors took me aside and told me there was nothing more they could do. He said he was in God's hands. That is when I remembered the dream I knew there was, an answer. I prayed to God and about an hour later, they said they would take him to another hospital.

I started to pray and I prayed to his loved ones and his Mom, because he was close to her and he loved her very much. I asked her to guide him.

It was about ten p.m. and this doctor, who was going to do the surgery, said, if he goes through the chest, Frank, would be paralyzed and a vegetable for the rest of his life, because he, had an aneurysm of the aortic.

The surgeon left and I was in the waiting room. It was about 3:00 a.m. I went down this hallway to the ladie's room and on the way back I saw this room number that I saw in the dream. All I could think of is that I was glad this wing was not open.

The surgeon came into the waiting room around 4:30 a.m. and said it was over.

A few hours later he started to bleed, so I went to the chapel to pray to God. He made it this far, please help him through this. I prayed to his Mom to guide him and watch over him.

A few hours went by and I went back to the waiting room. I was told the bleeding stopped.

The doctor told me he needed triple bypass, but he would have to do it another time. He said this was the worst surgery he ever did. A few weeks later they opened this wing and I was told they were going to move Frank there. So I went back down to the chapel and started to pray.

I said to God, no matter what he did in life, he should not have to suffer and if he goes in this wing he will die. You brought him this far.

Don't take him home with you now.

When I got back to the floor, maybe three hours later, the nurse told me something came up and we cannot move him.

You talk about power through prayer.

He came through it, but he was on a ventilator so long, he lost some of his voice. His vocal cords were paralyzed.

He did go through a lot while he was in the hospital. One night he pulled all his leds and was outside in his night gown at 1:00 a.m. One of the ladies that worked at the hospital, was just coming home so she helped him. With all the medication he was on, he said he wanted to come home.

You don't want to know my thoughts.

At one time they thought he had a stroke, but through the grace of God he pulled through it again.

One day we were sitting in the lounge and he had tears coming down from his eyes and I said what is wrong? He said his Mother, came to him. I said I was praying to her to

49

guide you and he said this beautiful light that he saw and his Mother, wanted him to go with her and he said "no, he was not ready." He said she came back to him and said she would say a rosary for him.

I told him, she was there to guide you and did you thank her for being there with you.

I told him, the light he saw his Mother in, is the light we came from. I said it is beautiful and peaceful.

Frank, started a novena, but never talked about death. It was a touchy subject with him. Why, I do not know.

Just as he never believed in physics or yoga, what ever, I did, but he never took the time to understand it.

I always felt in my heart he knew it was good, because the doctors and staff said "Gayle, is so positive."

My dear friend, who adopted me in her heart as her daughter, was physic. One time she told him to sit down and she wanted to do a reading for him. He told her that is b.s. She told him things I thought he might even pass out or fall off the chair. She told him he was not going to sell the restaurant the next day, and he told her your are ------ He did not sell the next day but he sold for months later just like she told him. (She always said the lord's prayer before she did a reading)

She told me she would come back to me through a trumpet. As it has been said, when the last trumpet sounds, this great being will walk the earth plane. Maybe this is when we will meet again.

After Frank got home, he got blood clots in both legs, so he was back in the hospital for more surgery.

Six months later he had triple by-pass. Later on he had to go through double by-pass.

I had to deal with a lot of problems, but all I could do was cling to God for support. I still did yoga and meditated. At times, yes, I was tired. Frank needed a lot of care and be nurtured back to health.

Again he needs more heart surgery. A few years later he was getting pains in his back and he was told it was arthritis, but it ended up to be another aneurysm in the stomach.

Then he had a bleeding ulcer from some of the medication he was on.

Eight months later he fell on the ice and broke his femur bone, and his heart doctor said he could not have any more surgery because he would not make it. But they said you cannot live with a broken bone.

They did the surgery and he stayed over a month in the hospital for rehab. After months, he was told his leg was not healing and that he would need more surgery. So I prayed and used spiritual healing. A year and half went by and the doctor said we had to come in to set him up for surgery. After the xrays were taken, he said he was amazed the bone healed and I told him, through prayer and healing. He said he was going to use his xrays to teach others.

His problems were not yet over. He was just to the doctor because he could not breathe and he was on medication for it. But that night in bed, he told me he had to go to the hospital. I called 911, and I said we were at the doctor's this morning but now he cannot breathe. This man I talked to, said, if your doctor, did not do anything, neither can we.

I don't know how he did it, but he got like a second energy and I got him to the hospital. He had pneumonia, and was in cardiac arrest.

Right after he got rid of the pneumonia, he started to get pulumonary fibrosis. Two months before he died, the doctor took xrays and said some parts of his lungs were getting better. I told this doctor, I was using spiritual healing on him.

His doctors, were loving and caring, and very great and had a lot of compassion.

They used to call him the bionic man, but they said I kept him here and it was all the good care he got. That is why he lived so long. No, it was God's will, not mine, for keeping him here. Like he said, he was not ready to leave this world.

One doctor even asked me to pray for his wife.

I pray every day God will guide doctors and their staff.

Frank's lungs got worse. He was back in the hospital and I was told he would have to go to a nursing home, because I would not be able to take care of him. It tore my heart apart, so I called this nursing home where I volunteer, at and they got a room for him the next day. I remember the doctor, said, "how could you get a room right away?"

It was on a Saturday, when he was moved to the home. I took him home on Sunday and I told him, if I can handle you, I will take you home. While he was home, he wanted to go back to the home, and come back with me the next day.

The next day I could not get out of bed. I could not move; I felt very sick, so I told God, I cannot take him home and I am never going back to the nursing home. You have to take care of him.

I argued with my self for hours that everything I went through with him. I can't handle this. I thought don't lose it. Don't let everything I have done, now go down the drain. I was stronger than that. I crawled out of bed. I felt like I was going to faint. I forced a piece of toast down. Got dressed and went to the home.

When I got there, he was lying in bed and he never said anything to me about coming home.

Three days before he died, I was leaning over his bed and I started to leave my body and I had Frank's hand. I was ready to take him to the other side. I said to myself, I can't do this. This is something he has to do on his own. It was, I did so much for him that I was going to take him home.

I got a call from the home at 11:00p.m. and they said they could not arouse him. They said he would have to go to the hospital. I said should I go, because I was always with him and they said no.

About 3:a.m., the hospital called and said what they were doing with him, and was that ok with me. I said just as long as he is not in pain.

I started to pray and fell into a deep sleep. The phone rang about 6:a.m. It was the hospital. They told me he passed away.

I called my sister and she said she would meet me at the hospital. We were taken into the room he was in, and I said to myself that is not him. I just stood there looking at him. He looked like an angel. I kept saying to my sister, just look at him, he looks like an angel.

Frank's eyes were half open and his mouth was like a circle, as if he were saying 'OM'.

He looked so pale. I sat down and I could not take my eyes off of him. A half an hour must by, but it seemed like moments. I just kept saying, look at him, he looks like an angel. He had this brilliant aura around his face. It just glowed. I wanted to kiss him and I wanted to touch his face but I knew if I did, my hand would have gone right through his face.

I knew his Mother came to him and took him to the other side. He was home with God. He was so attached to this world.

I touched his arm. I could not believe the aura around his face. But I remember my friend always told me, never touch anyone from the spirit world because they could give you a heart attack. But this was just an aura around his face.

I told my sister it looks like he is going to say something. If he does, I will drop dead right now. It is just that he pulled through so many things, anything is possible.

If he would not have died, I would have taken him home, if it took every ounce of energy out of me.

'Angels are made on earth not in heaven'

I never saw death coming for him. I never said goodbye. I know he is with me and we will meet again.

He already came to me and he told me they were taking care of him. I saw it in a dream. He was a young man, but still in physical form.

I had services for him, but it was only a Lodge of Sorrows. It was a club he had joined over thirty years ago. He told me you, had to believe in God, with this club, as they do a lot of good for others.

Most of his family did not like me because of our age difference, and who knows whatever was in their thoughts. My family liked him from the first time they met him, and greeted him with love.

After the Lodge of Sorrows, the members came up to me and each one had something to say. It was overwhelming. It touched my heart.

I know that God is with us and so are our loved ones, who keep sending us blessings. All you have to do is listen.

You can live with a person, fifty, hundred years and still do not know them.

After the services, we went to this restaurant that I know and my sister told me none of his family was coming. Only four of his family showed up.

I was standing and all of a sudden I could not move. It was like a fifty pound weight dropped from my waist down into the ground and from my waist up, I started to levitate. A few moments went by and I came together, and all I said kind of loud, "I waited thirty years for this day and do I feel good." I wanted to celebrate.

As I always told him, the day you die, your family will never talk to me.

His family will never know the beautiful death that he had.

I just have to keep my heart and divine mind alive and thank God.

'He was a stubborn, loving soul'

I am sure, he is experiencing higher levels of illumination and enlightenment, since he did not experience it here. As we know, this life is not our permanent home.

One of his sisters called me from time to time, and when she passed on, I saw her in a dream go to the other side with grace.

Meditation

Prayer is the question; meditation is the answer.

Every moment belongs to you whether you are living or dead. Let every moment be the love of God. Go on an inner journey. Let everything become love. Become one with God. You will experience something great, great things will unfold.

When you chant, (Praying) 'OM' everything springs from this word. Your life will be fulfilled. This energy is like a bolt of lightning; you will go higher and reach eternity. You do not have to make any effort. Everything will just happen naturally.

Time, you have to bend. Time is great. This one moment contains your life. Whatever you do is the right time. You don't have to chase it. You can be happy in any situation. This is oneness with time.

Don't dwell on your problems. They will just magnetize, get bigger and bigger and get out of control.

God has lifted people out of situations, they thought they could never get out of. Through meditation, you can be lifted higher and higher.

Meditation is inner contemplation where there is absolute silence. In this absolute silence, there is peace; in this absolute silence there is everything.

When you sow your practices, do it with all your heart and you will see how it bears fruit.

If you want to be sure of any decision you make, meditate and ask yourself, yes or no. The answer will come from within, as long as you are in accordance with God's will.

Man dwells in spirit where truth and love reign.

If you have been seeking for something and not yet found it, meditation is the way.

The image a person makes of himself, is called the ego. When the mind is restless and impetuous, it's like trying to harness the wind.

If you cannot control the mind, you will find it difficult to attain divine communion. But if controlled, he can attain the right means.

Meditation - you become one with the object of his meditation. It will keep him in harmony with others.

Work is a form of meditation.

You don't have to look for God, he is within you. Meditation will keep you in harmony with God.

The knower, the knowledge and the known, become one. Ways to control the mind.

Raja Yoga, Hatha Yoga implies mastery of the self. It is a spiritual discipline.

Kundulalini Yoga is Spiritual Energy

Having faithlessness and doubt, you destroy the self. God is forever at your side so evil can't touch you.

Do everything with enthusiasm. Mind is the source of all movement. See everything as harmonious action. Consciousness in action, be content and tranquil, merge with the absolute, God.

If you have false knowledge and suffer from delusion, you lack in wisdom.

Turn your enemies into friends and God will surely come looking for you.

Truth is God and God is truth. The mind and the breath are connected. One affects the other and you will achieve mental equipoise and inner peace.

Mantra Repeat this Sared mantra. The word mantra, is derived from the root 'men' meaning to think. Mantra is a sacred prayer or thought, repeated over and over and full understanding of its meaning. Praying with a full heart gets the fruit of his actions.

As some people repeat the rosary over and over.

Through yoga, you will reach enlightenment.

Guru (master) The relationship between a Guru, like a parent and child. A Guru is free from egotism.

When you repeat the word of God, it reveals what is hidden within. There is so much to know. Go within and experience love, repeating: "God and me, me and God are one."

I am perfect in God. A power goes through the body.

Make your life simple and anything you need will come at the right time. Everything is perfect and harmonious.

When you hoard things, it shows a lack of faith in yourself and in God.

With meditation, you will be more content and have tranquillity. Mind is the product of thoughts. All creation is God.

Chanting. Chanting, you always chant God's name in another form. People sing and chant. When you chant, the nectar flows through the body. When you meditate, it stops you from illusion. This world is only an illusion or dream.

Chanting is to still the mind and experience the divine love and wisdom in your heart. "OM" is a universal word, keeps you in tune with the universe.

Most scared of Mantras or words of Aum or OM (Power) Considered as the name of God, and a source of all Vidration, which pervades life, the sound in meditation to purify and align the various parts of the personality, and to stimulate psychic centers.

"Siddha Yoga Meditation," Zen, Shambhala

Sit in a comfortable upright on a chair or sit on the floor, with a pillow or blanket under you.

Repeat the mantra, or say a prayer, or OM Namah-Shivaya

'I honor the self within!

Focus your attention on the mantra, or just do some breathing in and out through the nose. Keep your attention on the breath. Let go. Allow yourself to become absorbed in it and glide into meditation.   If your thoughts and feelings or noise arise, just let it go. Bring your attention to the sound of the mantra.

Throughout the day mentally repeat "I am".

Repeat love 100 times a day

I am light and love at my core,

I am all, I am well.

Repeat God's name one minute out of every hour. It will put you on a higher spiritual plane.

God and me, me and God are one. Repeat this fifteen times a day. Go deep inside yourself. Find the space within. Let nothing else come to your head, but your own inner space. No matter how much money or friends you have, if your don't have yourself, nothing else really matters.

When you have your own inner self and truth, you have something to hang onto without being lost.

What is the self? What you see, unless it is God's will or God wants to take it away. You can never lose yourself; you will find the truth. Don't separate yourself from God or the world.

Lose the ego, find the truth. God is much greater than our foolishness. Self reformation you already have it. You experience ecstasy. Let it happen. Everything comes from your own inner soul.

The way you see yourself makes all the difference. Accept your own inner self. If you keep yourself clean on the inside it will show on the outside.

Become liberated while you are alive. Don't take life for granted.

Meditation is a state, identical to the state of yoga. Everything we experience is the self. You experience the world, but realizes it's true self. Self realization.

The most important is to make the effort to begin to practice meditation.

The body and mind are constantly moving all the time; this way we experience ourself as who we really are.

Everything in our lives is a manifestation of our thoughts. You can think ugly, envious, or good thoughts. Meditation will bring enlightenment.

When you meditate, try to pick the same time of the day or evening; try to pick a quiet place. Start with ten minutes and work up to twenty, or as long as you feel relaxed and at peace.

Sit in a comfortable position. Close your eyes, enter into silence, take a few deep breaths. (through the nose) Feel stillness throughout your meditation. Let the breath go; simply abide into silence. You will awaken the inner self and become in tune with infinite Universal One. You will find you will have a better and happier life. Just take the time and let nature take it's course.

You can say a prayer or God's name. You can use incense; music is beneficial. You open yourself to the unseen forces surrounded of beauty and grace.

Nothing comes but pure consciousness, the absolute God. We discover in meditation.

They have meditation centers and they are free, or you can get a teacher, but you might have to pay for it.

The first time I meditated, I was calm for three days.

It is very effective. After a few minutes stop. Your mind will become still, tune into the self. Now you have perfect silence, complete awareness. You experience the self, it is beyond conceptualization or imagination, it is the creations of the self, existence.

When you give up all thinking, you are left with conscience. When you give up all desires, you are left with a state of bliss.

Candle Gazing

Some people can't sit still, but if you try candle gazing, this can help you.

Sit on the floor in a dark room. Sit so you are eye level with the candle. Try to keep your eyes on the flame. Let your eyes become wider and wider. Watch the flame for ten minutes or half an hour. Close your eyes and focus on the flame. If it leaves, bring it back. Till you cannot see it any more.

Press the heels of your hands over your eyes for about one minute and you will see the light within you.

The light that you see when you meditate, is not from a candle or light bulb. It is from within.

When you meditate, you move beyond the waking, dream and deep sleep states; you go to the transcendental state. The Blue Pearl. When you see this little blue light in meditation, understand this is the form of the inner self. You can see the blue light. The Blue Pearl, a dot the spiritual center in the crown of the head. It is the body itself; all consciousness is contained in it. The waking and sleeping state.

Begin on learning the science of meditation, to set the foundation to achieve levels of illumination, relaxation and inner awareness.

Don't let your energy run backwards. If you have not achieved what you want in life, it could be due to restricting mental blocks or fixations, which could retard your advancement and could bring failure

Awaken your true self to a higher awareness and psychic unfoldment, so you have control over your life and the world. Meditation can release quiet, fears and help free yourself to a richer and happy life.

Self-Realization can put you on a higher level of life with incredible, peace, love, joy and power.

Become Free Born and free yourself of bondage and unite with Universal harmony and love and the force and power that creates and sustains the universe.

If it is not natural and it is not real, everything natural comes from God. God is all action expressing itself.

Don't be discouraged, have courage.

Because you keep your mind on God, doesn't mean you can't have fun. You will have more fun because you can laugh at anything. Everything will come naturally.

People are attracted to my aura and they will be attracted to yours too. Mostly men.

When you meditate, it comes from your consciousness and what you feel is your own completeness.

'When you are spiritual everything comes to you'

God made us capable to control the mind.

Know God and be at peace.

Special Stories

I would like to share a few stories with you.

I have been blessed with universal insights and wisdom, but the feelings I get and what I say, I have no control over it.

It is always good, so I know it comes from God.

At one time I could have left my body. I was in bed in the middle of the night and the choice was mine, but my Mom said she wanted me to stay until she leaves first.

Then I thought of my husband, who would take care of him. I could have been selfish and left but it would have been hard on my husband. So I stayed. I am glad I did. Now I can share all this with you. Maybe some day we will all meet.

A well known person came to me at 6:30a.m. He told me to bless this country and where I live. When I opened my eyes I could feel his presence leaving the room.

When you talked about loved ones in the spiritual world, Edgar Cayce, they will help you, they are closer than what you think.

Write them a letter let them know how you feel and anything you are hanging on to.

You will feel much better and you will feel a great difference in yourself. Because we think too much of our selves and our bodies and are too attached to this earth plane, when it is only matter. Liberate yourself from fear of death.

Instead of grieving, rejoice. Instead of sorrow, joy.

Through our grace and love we will meet again and again.

One person said to me, can you tell me when I am going to die? I told her to have more faith in living than in dying.

A very great person, who was to have their organs uplifted and needed surgery, had to go through some tests first. They found out that she needed to have four by-passes first.

Then she was told she would have to go to a nursing home. I told my Mother two days before her surgery, that if something good does not happen, she will take her life.

I went over to her house and we had dinner together the night before she had to go to the hospital. I got up to leave and she said I have to show you what I got in the mail. It was an S.S.I. card. Her name was on it but not the right number. So I called S.S.I. and they said it is a mystery to them.

She looked up in an old book and found it was her husband's number. I had the card in my hand and I was going to leave when all of a sudden I was full of all this energy. My whole body was just filled with energy and a tingle, in my right arm. I could have moved anything.

I said, "Your husband is with us. Do you feel his presence?" I repeated this a few times. I said, "can't you feel his presence?" and she said "no." I took her left arm and she automatically stood up right in front of me, like levitated.

While holding her hand I saw her face, like get long. She transformed right in front of me, like everything she was hanging onto left her body. I took my hand away and she sat down, and all she said was "why did he wait so long." Pills were not a way out. We never talked about pills.

She said, I will have the two surgeries and I will go to a nursing home. She was happy with her self.

I told her that is why I stay on a spiritual path. She said don't ever change.

When I got home that night I went to bed and all of a sudden I felt like celebrating. I felt so good, like I was on this high. This inner energy and bliss I had.

But it was not my glory, but God's. I was just greatful for the help she got and how it changed her life.

Less then a week she was home, and I told her I do not feel guilty that I did not get up to see her and she said that was ok, all my loved ones were with me.

A good friend of mine, who passed away, adopted me in her heart, as her daughter. As before, I told you she will come back to me through a trumpet. And she told me, Angeline, an angel, will guide me.

Another beautiful lady, told me she read this book that this person died and came back, and it was about an angel and everything in the book I already told her.

This is a very special person. For many years she had negative thoughts about herself and her life. Of all the years she was on different medications, Valium, Librium, alcohol and more. She ended up going to different hospitals and rehabilation centers.

At one time she stopped the alcohol and some of the medication. She was always asking God to help her. She even moved up north, hoping that this would change her life and things would get better.

Months later she got her first anxiety attack. She was put on Zanax, an anti-depressant pill.

Things got worse, and she ended up in a physic ward. After nine days the medication was changed. She stayed two more weeks. She tried biofeedback and other theraphy, for the next two years.

One person was told by doctors, that he would never walk again. Now he swims, walks, works and does much more. He changed his thoughts into positive ones.

The doctor should heal the patient mentally with the first visit, so when the patient leaves, he would be healed.

I don't know if it is still true today, but in this one country, if the doctor did not heal the patient with the first visit, the patient did not have to pay.

He that believeth in me, the works that I do, shall he do also greater works.

We can all heal ourselves and others. We are just a channel or a link between God and the universe.

After the two years, this new psychiatrist gave her an overdose. She ended up in the hospital. At this time she even asked God to take her life.

In 1995, she moved back to her home town. She was still having the anxiety and still depressed. She checked into a hospital to rid herself of addicting drugs and the use of cognitive therapy. It took her every minute and hour just to get through the day. The end of 1997, she said she is going to take control of her life and if I would help her through it. I kept her very busy so her mind was off her problems. She needed spiritual guidance which comes from God, as I am only a channel, between God and the universe. She went off the medications. She started yoga and swimming. She uses herbs.

She has changed her whole attitude about herself and life. As soon as she gets a negative thought, she changes it to positive right away. She never lets a lack of anything stay a moment with her, so it does not bring her any sorts of disease or difficulty. She now has a sexual life with her husband, who is very supporting and now she can even cry.

People say she glows, and she knows God, is right there for her

I Love Her

Shes My Sister

My Sister is now a Reiki master

Conclusion

Life is without beginning or end.

We are all connected in some way, so we should see God in each other.

Awake to you own inner consciousness, know the self.

Have faith, everything is all-right.

Think well of yourself and others.

Protect us from all forms of ignorance.

If God is for us, who can be against us.

Pray for your own soul.

Walk by faith, not by sight.

God is your strength and your shield. He is right there meeting your every need.

Take refuge in the lord.

Give all your problems to God.

Keep your life spiritual.

Accept everything in life as a gift, because some day you will have to give it back.

It is time to be creative; create inner happiness and harmony.

Be joyful and contented. Love life every day and you will become more content and happy.

Get rid of man-made laws and apply God's laws.

Life is God.

If you think it, you can do it.

Apply God's spiritual laws; spiritual enlightenment; have a clear vision and understanding God's direction.

After reading this book and you want to change your life, please get a good teacher, master to guide you along a spiritual path.

Use what God gave you. He gave you his kingdom, and to free yourself of bondage, fear, sin, grief loneliness, etc. You have the right to be free from all of the above.

Any desires you have pray, to God. He answers all prayers.

When you reach a higher state, you will be completely happy and satisfied with your life. You will not be in need or want of anything. Great things will just happen.

Rise above material conditions.

Do not go to a mutitude of places. Go to the source. God.

There are no secrets in God's kingdom. Everything comes from above and everything comes from God.

As it all comes from within.

Plant a seed and watch it grow.

Through my eyes I see everyone special and perfect.

You have a choice in life, but you cannot serve two masters.

Destroy material beliefs and have only spiritual beliefs.

Everything is a state of mind, but through the grace of God, all things are possible. 'Believe'

The greatest miracle on earth is man.

God made me special. That I know. It comes from up above. He loves me more than I'll ever know. My Father's thoughts have touched my soul.

When you have faith, everything is possible without unselfed love.

I can speak from experience. When you conform to God's laws, everything will unfold. Destroy human beliefs and apply spiritual laws to every facet of your life.

The purpose of this book is to guide the wills of man.

Don't let your senses lose sight.

God is the only mind that can heal.

Let God's will become your will.

God is all and all is God.

Let all your problems be still.

When you are spiritual you know everything.

Fill yourself with peace and love.

Don't be a mental fossil.

Start you new journey, with spiritual growth and grace, meekness and good deeds.

Meditate, know God and you will know yourself.

'We need universal love'

If you want to walk in someones foot steps, Walk in God's!

Rid yourself of fears that you are hanging onto, and you will be healed.

The Time Is Now

Work on letting go of the past. Know you have everything,

Know that this is a new time and a new beginning.

Open your heart and speak only with love from it.

Be filled with light and love and know we are the light of the world.

Let there be peace and no more darkness; only the light of Reality. Have forgiveness and understanding.

Know that God is healing this planet earth. Everything is perfect and harmonious.

Let the healing take place and guide the wills of men.

We are the light of the world; we are living in the light of God. We are in perfect light right now. Only we can restore this plan on earth.

Keep light thoughts and light form.

Let the light banish darkness forever.

It is time to walk in the light.

God Loves You And So Do I

I am grateful for Edgar Cayce and all the good he has done for others and myself.

When he came to me in that dream, he told me to bless this country and where I live.

Diet, attitude, meditation, is a state of mind, so don't waste your energy on negative things; use it for only positive things

With out God, I never could have written this book.

I hope to see all of you and those in the spiritual world, in the new kingdom.

When you cry, you are alone. When you smile, the world smiles with you!

Close your eyes, smile into your eyes, open your eyes, and smile into the world.

This world is only an illusion. Wake up to your own inner strength and courage.

This book is for those who want to change their life by changing the negative into positive.

What changed my life. I stopped myself one day and said "there has to be more to life then getting up, going to work and going out to party," and there was.

Your mind is a very powerful tool; a very powerful weapon, as long as you use right action, not wrong action

Reverse your thoughts and thinking beliefs.

Just by changing your thinking, from negative to positive, your whole life will change. We should judge no one but our selves.

Ask God to take over your life and do something good with it.

If you have not achieved what you want in life, you have restrictions or mental blocks, which can attract failure or bad luck or accidents or spiritual growth. Exercise meditation can open the way for awareness and psychic unfoldment. This can release anger, fear, guilt. Free yourself don't be enslaved. You can live a rich and happy life.

You can make a book up with these thoughts, or a diary, and say them everyday or make your own up.

I would like to leave you with some thoughts, and hope you will start a new life with being positive at all times and see good in your self and others.

Starting with Edgar Cayce, he has many good books out and I hope you will get to read them. He was, and still is, a great being. Through our grace and love, I am sure we will meet, because every thing is possible.

I would like to start a center to be with people who would like to change their lives but there is the A.R.E. clinic that has groups where you can just meditate and great things will come to you, or just do some yoga. For diet, use your state of mind.

Start every day. Unfold peace and harmony. Walk with love. See good in others and the universe.

Know you are free from Karma, mentally affirming "I AM GOD" in the back of your mind, even if you think you are a mortal being. If you are a God you are free.'

Being present from the body and more with God, sickness and disease will disapear.

Ask God to transform your thoughts and life completely.

Don't let your emotions control you or your senses.

It is a material world not spiritual, but you can have fun when you have spiritual powers; you shine like the sun and know all. You will laugh at life even though you think you shouldn't, but that is nature. You can be happy in any situation.

If you are sad you can repeat "IT IS NOT ME".

Using words or music are good for the soul; they vibrate the cells.

There is no fear in love. Everything you need is within you.

God planned your life, so don't interfere with it.

Your thoughts are more powerful than your words.

Like a tree, it takes time and is only a little seed. So plant a seed and watch it grow.

If you are troubled, repeat "PEACE BE STILL"

A lie is for a moment; the truth is forever.

Just as an animal in a cage, he has no choice, but you do.

If you around negative people, surround yourself with a white light and fill yourself with peace, love and harmony. You will repel negative influences from any source.

No matter what anyone has done in this life, no one deserves to suffer.

When you think of others as your idol and believe it, it is not "your true identity". Think of God and that you are made in his image and likeness.

When your life changes, know it is for the best. Like if you get fired. That may be good because something better will come along.

If your think people are changing, it is you. Everything comes from within.

Mistakes are blessings and you can learn from them, but if you do not learn from them, they will just get tougher.

Take a plant. When the roots are all together and you have to separate them so they can grow, it is just like life, or a child. You have to let him or her go.

If you have odds with someone, inhale through the nose and mentally inhale love from this person, and exhale your love to this person. You can do this three times and throughout the day for three days. You will feel better and this person will come up to you and say "I don't know what got into me."

Don't be attached or effected by this earth plane or your body.

If you have a problem, trust God with it and he will prove and reveal it.

Trust your own inner self and accept it.

Use thoughts of love to heal yourself and others.

Everything in the past died yesterday. Everything in the future was born today.

Start fresh and new every day

Every morning salute God, the sun and the earth, and keep in your mind on blue skies, sunshine and warm weather.

When you have spiritual powers, you will shine like the sun and know all.

Inhale through the nose; inhale love from the four corners of the earth. Exhale love to the four corners of the earth.

Be still and let God work through you.

Fear and anger block the circulation to eliminating channels and cause diseases

You have to rid yourself of all problems and what ever is going on with your life. So get rid of it "NOW" so you don't take it with you.

Put trust in your self and all your actions will bear fruit

Have freedom not enslavement.

Don't lose your cool. Know that all power belongs to your mind; no power belongs to fear, anxiety, whatever the case may be.

You don't have to come up with ideas. If you come up with an idea and if you feel something good inside and creative, that is God's job. Listen for answers, nuture your thought into expression that you can express creative ways. You are capable and filled with inspiration. Everything is possible to God, is possible for you.

Again, plant a seed of strength, courage, alertness, intelligence, peace, love, joy, endurance, courage and peace, and know that nothing can interfere with your work, singing what ever it may be.

Be present from the body and be more with God. See yourself in spiritual form and see a brilliant aura that repels all negativity

(I saw my self in a dream in spiritual form and I saw my body in physical form with this beautiful aura)

See God in each other. Accept others as they are.

Have faith everything is all right.

Have compassion. Bless every one, as this moment contains your life

Everything is powerless unless you give it the power to hurt you. When you see people perform or go visit someone in the hospital, you feel drained when you leave. That is because they take your energy.

It is how you think mentally when your health is bad, that is why you should change your thoughts right away to think of a beautiful garden or a flower.

Like the common cold, if there is only one cold, why is there not only one pill? (This is a negative thought, so I better change it right away.)

If you don't like your job or something is in your way, go with the flow not against it; merge with it and become one with it.

Stay grounded with truth and love and you will win, even if you have a health problem use these words.

Don't let your mind play tricks on you; know you are perfect and harmonious.

Don't separate your self from God.

Pray for more light.

Have compassion, not self pity; it will only cause you problems.

Know that God dwells within you as you.

Think of this world as a beautiful garden and everyone in it as a flower.

If you want a paradise, walk in the light of truth.

Peace will come when you worship God and the self more

When you look at the good in everyone, then you will only see good in your self

See your self perfect at all times and the world around you

When something negative comes in your mind, revise your thoughts.

Work out your own salvation.

If you caused a problem, only you can solve it.

Set your affections on things above and who you are.

Don't lose your identity, be liberated. You are a free thinker.

Know the truth about others.

No problem is greater then what you make of it.

Know the mind is strong enough to resist any thing

Pain is the past; everything is new now!

Divine love heals situations that seem impossible

Give all your problems to God.

God loves me and guides me moment by moment

When you get a thought, act on it and thank God.

Heaven and hell are a state of mind.

Know you are strong enough, wise enough, to never doubt your self again

"WAKE UP"

This World Is Only An Illusion

A friend of mine who was psychic, brought me up with Edgar Cayce. She said she would come back to me through a trumpet, as Edgar Cayce came to me in a dream.

Anyone can read this book and know when they get through reading, it can change their life from material to spiritual and still have a lot of fun in life, and more, seeing things and life in a better way, as we are a reflection of what we see in this world.

As we are waiting for the new kingdom to come, get on the right track now. It is time to change your life now! Changing the negative into positive, you are the master. You are in control, as no one has the power to hurt you or take anything from you even your joy. This moment contains your life.

There are no limitations to the imagination

Plant a seed and watch it grow; plant a seed of Hope and courage.

Take control of your thoughts and life, but watch your thoughts so they don't control you. It is your attitude how you think and how you feel.

Remove all fears and you will be healed. Do not put weight on your heart. What have you done to punish yourself that you keep hurting yourself. Don't feed your fears.

It is how you think mentally when your health is bad. Do not let those thoughts stay with you even for a moment, ZAP it out. Change the negative to positive right away.

Think of the mind as a shield, using the words truth and love, so nothing can enter the mind and do not let anything rise from within. Get rid of it, like getting rid of a pair of old shoes.

Just like losing weight, there are two words to use. Our bodies are only matter just like JESUS CHRIST proved it to us.

I asked God, who is this great being who is going to walk on this earth plane and I saw JESUS CHRIST in a dream.

Don't condemn others; instead bless them from the lord God of your being. Inhale your love to them and send your love. You will feel better and they will have something good to say to you.

Have trust in your self; every thing is possible.

Remember, this is God's world and we are only residents. We are a reflection of what we see. See people with your spiritual eye, not the physical eye. God wants only your own spiritual effort and he gave us the freedom to be free. We took birth and we have to live it out.

Know the truth about your self. We are the light of the world and only we can restore this world back to sanity.

103

This is the way to peace on earth for all, so let your love flow from your heart and forgiveness in your soul.

In Gods eyes, we are all special and no one is greater than the next. You have enough love in your heart to fill this entire universe. As human love is doubt and fear. BE STILL AND KNOW GOD.

Don't change the world, change yourself. We are the light of the world. God love you and so do I.

DRINK A CUP OF JOY IT IS TIME TO REJOICE

Enlightenment comes through meditation, yoga and prayer and staying on a spiritual path.

"NOW IS THE TIME"

Edgar Cayce told me in a dream to pray for this country where I live, and to pray for the tribes.

Every government leader and their nation should meditate, including now, Yogic Flying. It improves the quality of life for individuals and the whole world.

This one man I knew, told me many, many, years ago, his Mother used to pray with other people in this one room, and one day he walked in and they were all levitating.

There is so much suffering and problems in the world today, that we need our governments to help improve the life of the people and to educate them for all global administration.

We need world peace, prosperity, happiness, love and heaven on earth.

We all are connected in some way, so we all stay together to make this a better world, when the new kingdom comes, and Brotherly love.

Praying for peace to stop all the crime in other cities. Pray for governments that are never satisfied; pray that they will be complete and satisfied.

People should use their inner skills, knowledge and wisdom, instead of money and power, and natural laws. "Gods Laws"

"Now is the time to enliben ATMA – the self."

We need people who are strong, not weak, to run this world for all countries. We need global administration spiritual people who understand, because no one has to suffer any longer.

If our leaders would pray and meditate and use spiritual thoughts and ideas, they would have less stress, better health, improve their every day living, be more at ease and have trust in themselves and others. No more fear. The whole world would be "STRESS FREE" and would be full of peace, love and harmony.

We would not need any more armies. Wars would stop.

God gave us the gift of life and this is how we respect it.

God gave us the freedom to be free and the power to heal ourselves and the whole universe, and look how it is being treated; with no respect for others or themselves.

It is an insult to God, the way his universe is being used.

We see so many people with heart, stroke, clogged arteries, because of high blood pressure. But today it is getting more well known about t.m., transcendental meditation and yoga, including diet and exercise.

Some people are using biofeedback and just meditation. Many can cut their medication down, just by using the above.

Meditation can do more help then some medications.

"BREATH CURES ALL"

You should always stay calm and relaxed, no matter what happens. With yoga and meditation, it helps to reduce stress and depression as well as other health problems. Always helps to keep a good attitude about anything.

Change the negative into positive right away. Do not wait even for a moment.

All intelligence comes from God and from your consciousness; and mentally using words to heal or calm you. Words like peace, love joy OM Guru.

Let everything be natural and obey Gods laws.

All we have to do is listen and rest and use our bodies to discover ourselves and the intelligence that God gave us.

Everything is a state of mind, no matter what happens in this world. Be in a state of consciousness, be undisturbed; change the negative into positive. Put your hand in Gods hand and get going and be at peace.

This world is only an illusion. Wake up and you'll see this world is only a dream. So get on with your life and your dreams.

Sing a song of peace!

In the beginning, God created the heaven and earth and said, " let there be light."

Now is the time for a new beginning. We are a co-creator with God and is expressed through us. This kingdom is full of light, love, and peace and we all have to do our part.

We have to begin with ourselves, because God dwells in us and we and God are one, as God is all in all.

See only the spirit of God in every soul. We should say to everyone "I love you" and open up your heart and let the unconditional love pour out. Let it radiate from the center of your being.

Know you are one with the light.

Filled with the light.

Illumined by the light.

You are the light of the world.

Send forth this light to join the other lights, that there be one light. The light of the world.

Let the light of love, peace and understanding, flow across the face of the earth, and illuminate every soul in the shadow of the illusion. Where darkness was, let there be light.

Let it grow in every form of life.

Let there be one perfect life now.

Let us all be filled with light and love.

Let there be total oneness.

Let us all return to Godkind.

Let peace flow in every mind.

Let your love flow from every heart.

Let forgiveness be in every soul.

From the light of the world.

Let there be one presence and one power. God is healing and harmonizing this earth. Let all errors be dissolved let the healing take place; let this world be restored back to sanity, let the love flow and have forgiveness reign in every soul.

The sense of separation is no more; we are the light of the world.

Don't blame God, blame man. Man is destroying this universe.

We are ever one and ever whole; from God this perfect world was born, even if this world disappears from view, it will always be the same.

We are the light of the world. God is in control. He fills every space and illumines every race.

With every action we perform in life, should be with love and grace.

Plant a seed of love and trust and fill your hearts with peace and love.

We are love and peace becomes the way as all false beliefs dissolve for all the human race.

We are a reflection of what we see.

As love flows from every heart.

We are unchanging impartial love of peace.

As peace becomes the way for you and me.

"NAMASTE"

From my heart to your heart

"SHANTI"

PEACE

About The Author

Gayle is a self-realized spiritual person. She has a strong bond with herself; she looks at life with light and love through her eyes. She has dedicated her life to God and others. She says you are nothing less than light and love. She self-taught herself in many ways.

Gayle is a Yoga teacher. She volunteers at many places, as she received a special commendation award in recognition of significant contributions to community life in Wisconsin, She has been on National T.V. And has written a book on Epilepsy, which she donated to the A.R.E. clinic, the Edgar Cayce foundation. She has written and published poems, for which she received the editors' award. She is an activist in her community. Her missions never end.

She is an associate with one who was formerly of The Platters. Stephen King just wrote a book which has something about The Platters in it.

Gayle is writing a true story based on *Joseph and The Amazing Technicolor Dreamcoat.* She hopes her friend who is producer will do a movie on it, as well as one on Edgar Cayce.

She would like to write a yoga book in the future for anyone to do yoga and make it simple. She just wrote a book for the A.R.E. Press, Edgar Cayce Foundation.

Her friend wrote a song, and hopes everything will unfold at the same time.

God is the author, as God planned her life. Now it is time for it to all unfold.

Nine Months before her husband died she knew that something good was coming into her life. Her friend or angel Allison came to her in a dream and she feels she is guiding her and for the spiritual insights she has for others and her self.

Gayle knows it is Gods love and thoughts coming through her to help others. She says it is a gift and if you use it the wrong way you will lose it.

She says higher we can not look farther we cannot go.

Please except this book as a gift from God. God has blessed me over and over I know he will surly bless the fruits of your life to.

God is just waiting for you to talk to him your desires and prayers he answers all desires and prayers.

He will surely bless you as he has blessed me.

In God eyes we are all perfect.